WARBIRDS
WORLDWIDE

The World's No. 1 Warbird publication

NUMBER

GW00370578

Top (Michael Shreeve) The Fighter Collection's *Bell RP–63C Kingcobra made its show debut at the North Weald* Fighter Meet *resplendent in its new Soviet Colour scheme.* **Lower** (Anders K. Saether) The Scandinavian Historic Flight's *Douglas A–26B Invader N167B in the U.S.A. prior to its departure for Norway.* **Back Cover** (both Paul Coggan) **Top:** *Bob Colling's B–17G N93012 Nine O'Nine is one of Tom Reilly's* Bombertown *restorations and* **Lower:** *Bill Harrison in his twin rotor Piaseki helicopter hops over Connie Edwards PBY, Oshkosh '86.*

WARBIRDS
WORLDWIDE

Volume Two Number One

Founders:
Paul A. Coggan
John R. Sandberg
Henry J. Schroeder III

Director and Editor:
Paul A. Coggan

Financial Consultant:
Philip S. Warner F.C.A.

Chief Pilot:
Robb R. Satterfield
(Lt. Col., USAF Ret'd)

Photographers:
Robert S. DeGroat (USA)
Philippe Denis (France)
Jeremy K. Flack (UK)
Jack Flinn (USA)
Alan Gruening (USA)
Peter Liander (Sweden)
Robert Livingstone (Australia)
Ron Miller (USA)
Frank Mormillo (USA)
Richard Phillips (USA)
Michael J. Shreeve (UK)
William B. Slate (USA)
Thierry Thomassin (Worldwide)

Editorial Address:
19 Highcliffe Avenue
Shirebrook
Mansfield
NOTTS. NG20 8NB
ENGLAND
Tel:
National (0623) 744476
International +44623 744476

WARBIRDS WORLDWIDE LIMITED
Company No. 2107572
Registered Office:
Winchcombe House
Winchcombe Street
Cheltenham
GLOS GL52 2NA

CONTENTS

WARBIRDS WORLDWIDE is published in book form every three months. It is the official publication of the organisation of the same name and acts as a permanent published record and a forum for the exchange of information and ideas amongst our membership. It is provided free of charge to members and is available at the cover price to non-members. Details of membership fees are available from the Editorial address: Membership is open to anyone with an interest in warbirds and warbird ownership is not a qualification required to join.

WARBIRDS WORLDWIDE BRIEFING

Peter Thelen's magnificent Chance Vought Corsair N179PT/Bu. No. 122179 on its first flight on 28th April 1988, after a two year restoration programme. Glenn Wegman did the fine restoration – his previous projects have included the Pete McManus Mustang N51PT and the Whittington Bros. TF-51D now owned by the Lone Star Flight Museum. Next stop – the paint shop. (Peter Thelen).

Exclusive they said. We had published two weeks earlier. Exclusive they declared. Warbirds Worldwide had covered the same subject nine months earlier. I had made a mistake, for like everyone I'm human and errors do occur – with the vast number of data and serials that are handled the occasional slip is inevitable. Within a month the mistake had been copied. I suppose that in a way we should be flattered. You will no doubt notice that we have announced Warbirds Worldwide is the *World's Number One Warbirds Publication.* That is not an arrogant statement: it is based on what you, the readership are telling us, and we have almost a thousand letters on file saying just that. The standard is set, and with each issue we try to make improvements and hope you enjoy the results. As an organisation, Warbirds Worldwide is also gaining strength. Some people are under the impression that it is an organisation solely for warbird owners. *Not so.* It is for *everyone.* The President of *EAA,* Paul Poberezny hit the nail squarely on the head in a statement he made in 1985: "When one looks back at much of aviation, it is not, unfortunately, always the pilot or airplane owners who makes possible the activities that we enjoy and

benefit from. Let us not forget those who are dedicated to our cause. Those who sit on the perimeter just wanting to be accepted and be a part of us." When I set out to get Warbirds Worldwide off the ground those words echoed all around. They still do.

There are those that will try and tell you that warbirds are for the very rich only. True, a healthy bank account smooths the passage, but there are many owners who either operate a smaller, lighter warbird or are part of a syndicate operating a piece of heavy metal. People can participate in many other ways. There are a lot of volunteers around who give a lot of their valuable time to helping rebuild or maintain a warbird. We hope that our publication has achieved one of its aims at least. To illustrate the amount of work that goes into rebuilding warbirds. For across the world there are hangars and workshops full of airframes, many not even resembling an aircraft, being rebuilt. Our membership alone are rebuilding some 42 warbirds. Skill, engineering expertise and sheer hard work are all ingredients going into these rebuilds. But most of all – it is the dedication that binds the warbird people together, and it triumphs when the aircraft concerned takes to the air.

We are pleased to announce the publication of our first Special Edition: MUSTANGS WORLDWIDE. It follows the same format as this journal, and we are planning several more, the next of which will be published in October. For Warbirds Worldwide Number Six we have a very interesting line up including coverage of the French warbird scene. For those who would like first hand experience of this aspect I strongly suggest you make a serious attempt to attend the Warbirds meeting at the Aerodrome de Douai-Vitry on June 10th, 11th and 12th. There are some 37 warbirds scheduled to appear (more details on page 41). Warbirds Worldwide members can get in *free of charge* on presentation of their membership cards, and landing charges will be waived on the 12th if you wish to attend by air. Short notice but one worth making the effort for. On with Number Six – see you there!

Paul A. Coggan 17th May 88.

WARBIRDS WORLDWIDE

Scandinavian Historic Flight A-26B Invader –

Anders K. Saether's Douglas A–26B Invader 44–34602 arrived at Oslo Fornebu in early May after a ferry flight from the U.S.A. The aircraft was acquired from Stahlman Farms who had owned it since it was phased out of service with the USAF in 1961. The aircraft was refurbished by *West Star Aviation* who took over the entire *On-Mark* Invader inventory of spares. Registered N167B the Invader was painted by Goodner Brothers of Mena, Arkansas, in a Korean Theatre paint scheme, that of the 729th Bomb Squadron, 452nd Bomb Group. As well as having an eight gun nose section fitted the aircraft also has new cockpit glazing installed and a new avionics fit which includes LORAN.

The aircraft is available for airshows in Europe and those interested should contact Warbirds Productions on (0623) 744476. More on this, including air to air photographs in an early issue of Warbirds Worldwide.

Top: (Anders K. Saether). *All masked up for painting at Goodner Brothers in Arkansas.* **Centre:** *The team checking the paint part way through the respray.* **Bottom:** N167B in its new colours: Imron silver with red trim in 729th Bomb Squadron colours and with Scandinavian Historic Flight titles.

WARBIRDS WORLDWIDE

scheme. The forward fuselage was natural metal, leading edges of the wings were white and the trailing edges of the wings were adorned with six black and white stripes. Rear port fuselage was dayglo red and the starboard rear fuselage was green. This garish colour scheme had a practical purpose, being used to position different formations of aircraft on a particular section of the Mitchell camera ship. Upon arrival in Spain one of the film crew, upon seeing the unique paint scheme, remarked '. . . it's a damn great psychedelic monster . . .'. That nickname was to remain with the aircraft for the duration of the filming.

By mid March 1968 the team of RAF personnel at RAF Henlow had all but finished work on the Spitfires and Hurricanes. The airworthy aircraft flew out to Duxford, the taxiable and static aircraft following by road transport. Flying the Spitfires and Hurricanes for the film was a select band of Royal Air Force pilots, all qualified flying instructors with many hours on fighter type aircraft. All of the pilots underwent conversion onto type in one of the Spitfire T.9 dual control aircraft. Leading the pilots was Wing Commander George Elliot, who personally tested each pilot on type.

Undertaking the enormous task of maintaining the film fleet of warbirds was *Simpsons Aero Services* of Elstree. In charge was John 'Tubby' Simpson. Hamish Mahaddie recalls '. . . John Simpson was a first class aero mechanic and an expert on the Rolls-Royce Merlin engine. With RAF airmen undertaking first line maintenance (refuelling and flight line tasks), John and his team of civilian engineers kept the aircraft serviceable during the shooting schedule of the film. If we had an aircraft go unserviceable during shooting with engine problems for example, John would remove the offending part and off he would go to Rolls-Royce at Filton or Derby, or in the case of aircraft radiators, up to Dellaney-Gallay, the radiator specialists. The repaired items would be back on the aircraft by the following morning. All this was made possible with the use of film money. Sadly, John Simpson was not a man to delegate work and all the rushing about all over the country probably contributed toward his untimely death shortly after the film was completed. I had maintained that I would lose one aircraft per week due to unserviceability during filming and after twelve weeks we would have had no aircraft left to film. Due to the excellent work of *Simpsons Aero Services* we had no major serviceability problems whatsoever."

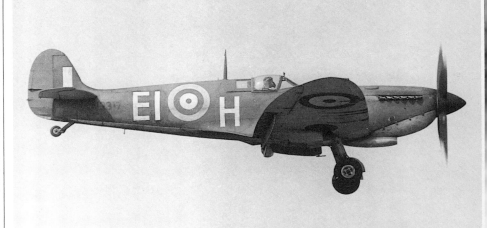

The scene was set . . . . *WW*
Robert Rudhall.

In Issue 6: Lights, Camera's, ACTION! Robert Rudhall continues with the second part of the story of the filming.

Top: (Adrian Balch) *depicts the Psychedelic Monster: B-25 44-31508 camera ship for the film.* **2nd Top** (Adrian Balch) *Buchon '11' at Duxford, August 1968.* **2nd Bottom** (Tony J. Clarke) *depicts Spitfire IX MH434/G-ASJV landing at Duxford 7th September 1968 and* **Bottom** (Peter R. March) *Spitfire T.9 at Elstree with Simpson Aero Services undergoing overhaul post filming. MJ772/G-AVAV, April 1969.*

Top: (Tony J. Clarke) *depicts Spitfire PR19 PM631 dressed as EI-K lands at Duxford after a filming sortie on 7th September 1968. The 'used' finished applied to all the aircraft utilised for filming is particularly evident in this shot, which contrasts with the state of most of the airframes of today.*

WARBIRDS
W O R L D W I D E

Tony Clarke's *picture of Hispano Buchon ex C4K–170/ G–AWHS coming in to land at Duxford in September 1968 makes a very nice contrast to* Michael Shreeve's *shot of the same aircraft at Duxford on May 12th 1988. Nick Grace has completely rebuilt the Buchon and once film work for* Piece of Cake *is complete the aircraft, now registered G–BOML will be painted to represent a Bf109 G–6.*

"the **Battle of Britain**"

The start of it all. Tom Reilly's first facility utilised this parking lot at Sleigh Boulevard, Orlando, Florida.

Bombertown U.S.A.

A visit to Tom Reilly's hangar on a Saturday afternoon reveals just as much restoration work and aircraft activity as on a weekday. *Bombertown, U.S.A.* operates seven days a week. Even on the weekend, the noise of 10 rivet guns and air drills combine with the roar of engines and blast of propellers to produce a racket that is deafening, yet beautiful. In fact, weekends may even have more activity than weekdays, since pilots and fly-ins keep the hangar area and sky filled with warbirds. On Saturdays and Sundays, an hour doesn't pass in Kissimmee without seeing a warbird coming from or headed to the Airport.

Tom Reilly is the centre of most of the activity at the facility. His office is located at the left entrance to the hangar. Most of the time, though, you won't find him in the office. He'll be in the hangar checking on sheetmetal work or inspecting an aircraft restoration. Other times he'll be on the ramp, looking over engine maintenance or surveying the collected aircraft parts, making mental notes of what's available and the various condition of the pieces. He named his hangar area *Bombertown, U.S.A.* after seeing the movie *Top Gun*. "In the film, one of the hangars at the base had *Fightertown, U.S.A.* painted on it," Reilly says. "Since I've always got seven or eight bombers hanging around, this has got to be *Bombertown, U.S.A.*"

Jack Flinn examines Tom Reilly's restoration facility at Kissimmee — *the* place to be if you are interested in Bombers.

At any given time, Reilly could have as many as 20 warbirds in or around his hangar. Centrally located in the state of Florida, Reilly's Kissimmee facility has become a very popular gathering spot for the warbirds. "People are always flying in on weekends," he says with a smile. "They park their airplanes here or have them worked on." Nearly every weekend Doug Shultz rolls his TF-51D, *Rascal III*, out of the hangar to give four or five hours of training. The Burch's, Selby, Scott and Bill, fly their T-6, P-51D, and PT-22's out of the Kissimme Airport nearly every weekend. Tom, himself, is usually airborne with the B-25 *Triple 7* giving dual instruction, readying someone for a checkride. Other weekend visitors include Jack Kehoe and Dennis Marcotte who fly over with their SNJ-5's. Their fly-ins are usually for minor aircraft work or simply to get fuel. Jack also gives dual instructions in his SNJ for advanced training, prior to a trip in Shultz's TF-51D. One or two aircraft from the *Valiant Air Command* or the *Wings of War* usually stop by each weekend, just to say "hi". Usually, Stearmans from Zell-

wood and Tangerine fly in, owned by Bob White and Jim Kimball. The aircraft come from two rural grass strips in Central Florida. Kimball's facility is located 35 miles northwest of Kissimmee. The Stearmans fly with Rick Thompson's Tigermoth, which is also based here.

Dr. Miles Douglass and Mitch Johnson can usually be seen shooting landings at the Kissimmee Airport in Miles' T-28. Between the private owners, the restoration shops along the east coast, the *Valiant Air Command* and the *Wings of War*, Florida is a bonanza of warbirds and warbird activity.

Tom usually has two dozen aircraft parked or being worked on at *Bombertown*. Each of the aircraft has its own story about outside activity and uses. Scott and Bill Burch's T-6 sits inside the hangar repainted grey with Japanese Imperial Air Force rising sun insignia on the wings and fuselage. The aircraft was used in filming two productions, one in North Carolina and the other in Pensacola, Florida. In Pensacola, the plane was used as part of *War and Remembrance* while the North Carolina filming was for the film *Too Young the Hero*.

Bob Collings has the most aircraft parked at *Bombertown*. A B-24 Liberator of his is being restored and the work is progressing very well. The wing and centre section should be complete by April 1988, and the fuselage should arrive at Kissimmee in May 1988.

A quick glance around the hangar reveals two PT-22's, three P-51's, five B-25's, one B-24, three TBM's, one F4U-5, one Tigermoth, three T-6's and a Sea Fury.

The Hawker Sea Fury is one of the 26 acquired from Bagdad, Iraq. The plane was first moved to the old Herndon Airport in Orlando, now known as Orlando Executive Airport, before being relocated to Reilly's own hangar. Aircraft parts and sections can be found surrounding Reilly's hangar area, both inside and out. Documenting the activities at Bombertown can be difficult, because pictures taken one week may not show what's going on at the facility the next, because so much work and restoration takes place there. Reilly has become a recognized figure in the Kissimme area, and has sponsored warbird fly-ins for the past three years. The vintage aircraft show has drawn large support from the local community, even though the weather hasn't been as cooperative as Tom would have liked!

"It has rained every year," Reilly recounts. "If Kissimmee ever needs rain, just call me and I'll plan an airshow. Sunday's seem to be the worst, especially this year," he says with a smile, thinking back on the weekend events of Jan. 1–3. "We were mostly inside the hangar on Sunday. We moved all the warbirds we could fit under the roof. The people still showed up." For Reilly's first fly-in, the hangar had not been repainted with his own logo and grass was growing through the cracks in the taxi ramp. It didn't matter, spectators arrived in droves to see the warbirds. They came from the local community and from towns and cities hundreds of miles away and have continued to come in larger numbers each year thereafter.

It's the unusual aspects of the restoration business that attracts Reilly, who says his calling is building things no one has built since World War II. "I enjoy building things that requires a lot of research and development," Reilly says, pushing back the baseball cap with aircraft insignia he always seems to be wearing. He takes off his glasses, cleans them and begins to list a few of the many pieces he's constructed. "I've done landing gear assemblies for a JU-52 and made wing attach angles for B-25's. That type of work, heavy duty machine shop work, is what I really enjoy. "I built a turret shell for a B-17 from scratch, and I've done Bendix top turret shells from TBM's and B-25's from scratch. I don't just rebuild them, I love to build them from scratch. And when my men and I build these things, we try to make them look *identical* to the original. That's what gives us pride. That's my real calling, the work I really enjoy."

Tom has secured a B-17G of his own. This was the one Boeing modified for Pratt & Whitney and had five engines. A turboprop was placed on the nose of the Flying Fortress for in-flight testing.

The aircraft was badly damaged by a tornado that went through Windsor

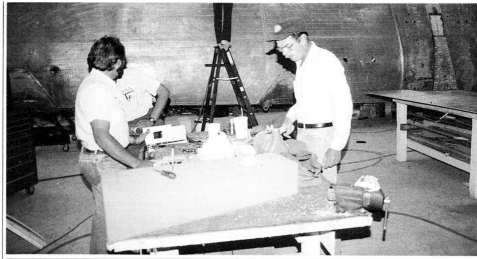

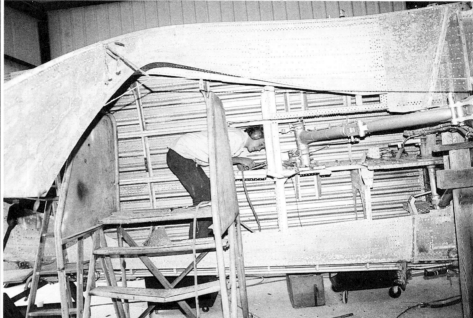

Tom Reilly (Right) giving advice on the overhaul of a part for the B-24 Liberator project. **(Top). Centre:** *The mainplane of the B-24 is enormous. One of* Bombertown's *engineers is seen here inside the wing replacing a bracket.* **Lower:** *One of the Mitchells – B-25J N898BW/45-8898 nearing the end of a 100 point restoration. Several more in the pipeline.*

Bombertown U.S.A.

Locks, Conn. about eight years ago. The bomber is coming to Florida from the New England Air Museum, and with the 365-days-a-year schedule at the hangar, work will begin on restoration as soon as it arrives. "We work at least 15 hours a day, seven days a week," Reilly says. "We all enjoy the work we do, and it keeps us going at a steady pace. Once a month on Sunday we usually have a cook-out for our own people and also invite all the warbird lovers in the area. We discovered that people fly in just to be with us. It's a fun time for everyone, though we still work on the planes and make sure everything's on schedule – even on Sunday."

The friendliness at Bombertown is apparent. Warbird lovers stop by Tom's place almost daily, keeping in touch with other enthusiasts who are interested in the aircraft. However, as Tom likes to say, "business is business and our work goes on from 7 a.m. until 10 p.m. six days a week." On Cookout Sundays, the crew usually work only half days, 7 a.m. – 7 p.m. What brings all these people together at *Bombertown, U.S.A.* in addition to seeing all the warbirds gathered in one place is the comaraderie and pride behind their work; dozens of people will stop by the place during the week. Most of them are warbird fans. Others are veterans of air battles fought over Europe or Asia decades ago.

In addition to his paid staff, Reilly will usually have numerous volunteers helping out around *Bombertown, U.S.A.* Many a visitor who has stopped by Reilly's place soon found himself, or herself, busy assisting with a restoration. Reilly has a reputation of putting people to work. He doesn't discriminate by sex, either. Most World War II aircraft were made by women since a larger number of the men were serving in the armed forces.

Women can be found working alongside men on the World War II aircraft that Reilly restores. In fact, sometimes the women working for Tom can do the hard-to-reach jobs that the men can't. "We have one helper who has a reach of – it seems – about five feet! We'll come to the end of the wing in a B-25 and need some help to buck rivets. She'll show up, stick her arm way up into the end of the wing and be right in position for the riveter on the outside. She sure is a help to use." Many wives of the old-timers know where to find their husbands on a weekend. The phone at *Bombertown* will ring, and a wife will be on the line asking for her spouse. "Once I had this man stop by the shop and watch me work on a B-17 top turret shell. He asked me what it was and I told him. You know, I think I have something that looks like that in my back yard," the fellow said. He convinced Reilly to go with him to Leesburg, about 75 miles north of Orlando. "We went into this junkyard," Tom explains, "that was littered with old wrecked cars. We started digging through the mess and even had to cut some of the grass back as we were searching. I know it's back here somewhere," the fellow said, so they continued to look through the debris.

"Then we saw it," Tom says, his voice becoming quiet as he tries to reconstruct what happened. "All of a sudden I saw this old glass structure. It was a glass

Top: *The B-24 mainplane again. Work is well underway on this particular project and the fuselage should have arrived as we go to press for similar treatment.* **Lower:** *Iraqi Fury N59SF/37755, ex WM484 is one of the warbirds stored awaiting rebuilding.* (Both Jack Flinn).

bomber's nose from a 'C' model B-25. It was in need of restoration, but was an excellent find. Now I wondered what the nose would cost me, so I asked him, 'would you sell this to me?' " "No, I won't sell it to you," the old fellow replied. "Then he took a long look at me, with an expression in his eyes I can't describe. I tell you what I'll do," the greying gentleman said, "I'll *give* it to you, if I can know for sure it'll go on an airplane that will fly again."

"I owe him dearly," Reilly says. "He's going to get the best ride in a B-25 he can imagine!" Visitors and tips such as that is only one way Reilly finds his restoration pieces. Reilly's success with warbird restorations is what makes *Bombertown*

grow. He's come a long way from Sleigh Boulevard in Orlando where he first began restoring a B-25 in an open field. Tom had a small fabrication shop and parking lot there. He was offered the chance to purchase the hangar at the Kissimmee Airport, and Bombertown was born.

With the move in operations, Tom had to face some rather complicated problems – how to move many tons of parts and a partially restored Mitchell from Orlando to Kissimmee. It took 40 trailer trips to move the parts. The solution for the bomber was to tow the aircraft down U.S. highway 441 for 23 miles in the middle of the night, in order to avoid the traffic. The move took four hours and was a task

Reilly never wants to repeat again.

Bringing the B-25 *Chapter 11* from New Jersey to Florida was slightly different. Tom travelled there to work on the bomber. The Mitchell was a derelict aircraft for eleven years in Caldwell, N.J. after having been used in filming *The Battle of Britain*. Reilly purchased the airplane in August of 1977 and had it ready to fly by February of 1979. I have flown as a passenger on that airplane in 1985 after an airshow and can remember Chapter 11 flying east to the Indian River, turning north to Titusville, then west for the return to the airport. As we flew over the water, passed the coastline and then continued inland to the final destination, I couldn't help thinking of a final destination of a different sort in 1942, when Jimmy Doolittle made his famous Tokyo raid in similar aircraft. It's history such as that of the vintage aircraft that Tom Reilly is preserving.

"My goal is to put together and save as many old airplanes as I can," Tom will tell you. "I want to restore and fly them, go to the airshows and let these veterans see once again the aircraft they flew during the war years." I am a first-hand witness to Reilly's success. It was several years ago, during a visit to an old auto salvage yard searching for parts when, in the distance, I heard the roar of four Curtis-Wright engines. One of my colleagues gazed skyward and said "what's that?".

"A B-17," I told him without bothering to look up myself.' Hearing the engines I knew it could be only one aircraft. "No", he protested, "there're not any more of them around." I smiled at him and

B-25 Chapter XII – looking very different to when it was configured as a camera ship for the film The Battle of Britain. *Tony Harmsworth Photo (see Page 12).*

pointed over to the Flying Fortress that was making a final approach to the Kissimme Airport. "Well, if you don't believe your ears, just take a look over there."

We both saw a beautiful sight as the B-17 came in to land, bathed in the soft orange-pink glow of the fading sunset. Several days later I saw television news coverage of the airplane. It was Bob Collings' *Nine O Nine* the restored B-17G. Tom did the restoration and it won "Best Bomber" award at Oshkosh in 1986.

It's after dark at Bombertown, U.S.A. when the last aircraft taxies in and is parked in the hangar. The few of us that

remain walk out of the enclosure with Tom, after he turns off the lights and Bombertown settles down for a well deserved night's rest.

We all will return in a matter of hours, though for the Sunday cook-out, and Tom be questioned about his next trip to pick-up or restore a warbird. Tom has travelled throughout the world to purchase and restore World War II aircraft and has been to such far-flung places as Europe, Southeast Asia, Canada, and 16 states in the U.S. Recognized as one of the top warbird restoration men in the country, Tom Reilly has put *Bombertown, U.S.A.* on the map.

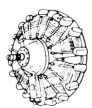

The Military Austers

Auster Mk.9 XN408 is currently based in Florida. It was originally supplied to the Far East for anti-terrorist duties and was later passed to the Hong Kong Air Force (Bill Fisher).

Bill Fisher takes a look at a more cost effective approach to the warbird scene with the smaller Military Austers.

Before I start I believe that I should give my definition of a warbird. Although some people are content to treat a warbird as being any aircraft that is operated in military service I believe the definition should be applied to those aircraft which have operated with the military, during a period of conflict, and in a conflict environment. This definition would therefore exclude the majority of accepted warbirds which were built to military contracts but came down the production line after the end of hostilities. (A point for further discussion? –Ed.)

I can already hear the American readership saying "what the hell is an Awster". Well, the pronounciation is OSTER. It is what the British call an Air Observation Post (AOP) and what the Americans call a Spotter. Historically it is related to the Piper J2 and the Taylorcraft Model B.

When C.G. Taylor left the Taylor Aircraft Company having sold his shares to W.T. Piper, he set up a company called Taylor-Young Aeroplane Company which later became Taylorcraft. There he designed the Taylorcraft B which was built under licence by Taylorcraft Aeroplanes (England) Ltd. in Leicestershire. That airframe was developed through the Model C to the Taylorcraft Plus D which was used by the British Army as the Auster 1. This was not an impressed civil aeroplane but an aircraft which from its concept had been seen as having a pos-

sible military application as a result of which the prototype T9120 was delivered to Old Sarum for military trials just before Christmas 1939.

During April and May 1940, the period of the so called "phoney war", Auster 1's were evaluated in France until returned to England in mid-May. The delivery of production aeroplanes commenced in mid 1942 and early deliveries were made to North Africa and saw service here and in Italy. Although Auster 1's were attacked by Bf109's the speed difference and manoeuvreability of the Auster 1 usually resulted in nothing worse than a few holes in the fabric. It will be seen however that as a type the aircraft saw genuine service in a combat environment.

The Auster II was not proceeded with and the Auster III was a conversion of the Auster I airframe to take the Gipsy Major I engine, thus increasing the horsepower from 90 to 130 hp. Deliveries commenced early in 1943 and these were also shipped to North Africa. Well over 450 Auster Mark IIIs were produced for army co-operation duties and at the end of the war substantial quantities of almost new airframes existed. As a result 56 aircraft

were transferred to the Royal Australian Air Force to receive serials in the A11-range. 58 aircraft were delivered to the Royal Netherlands Air Force, 20 went to Greece and 3 aircraft (MZ 232, MZ 235 and MK 129) became part of the post-war Czech air force. PH-UFM of J. Damms was painted up as RT607 for the film of *A Bridge Too Far* although the serial correctly belongs to a Mark V.

The first major redesign of the Auster airframe came with the Auster IV which featured a third seat for an observer in the rear cabin and the use of the Lycoming 0-290D engine. The major differences between the Mark IV and the Mark V was that the Mark IV did not have a full blind flying panel and was fitted with a vane type trimmer under the tailplane which was replaced by a conventional trim tab on the Mark V. Both marks saw service during the latter part of the war and a number of those which survived have documented history in a combat environment.

Probably the best documented history is that of G-AJXV which was a civil conversion from NJ695 which was exported to France and crashed in October 1963 whilst registered as F-BEEJ. It appears to have been rebuilt using a Mark IV fuselage as NJ695 now sports the vane type trimmer. NJ695 was delivered to C Flight of 661 Squadron and Pete Farries has extracted the following history from the squadron records.

AUSTER AOP MK IV (British Taylorcraft)

Constructed 1943	Construction No. 1065	Military No. NJ 695
17th Jul '44	Taken on charge 20th Maintenance Unit.	
22nd Sept '44	Issued to C Flight of 661 Squadron. Attached to Canadian 1st Army, who had followed up the Normandy landings. (Operating as artillery spotter).	
10th Oct '44	Operating on a front between Dunkirk and Antwerp, moving up through Belgium following Canadian 1st Army.	
8th Nov '44	Joined Canadian 2nd Army and went on to Nijmegan and Arnhem.	
8th Feb '45.	Operation *Veritable* (the drive through the Reichswald Forest and the Sigfried line supporting 2nd Canadians).	
19th Feb '45	C Flight moved to Cleeve and earned the distinction of being the first Flight to enter Germany.	
24th Mar '45	Operation *Plunder* crossing the river Rhine. C Flight with 2nd Canadians.	
31st Mar '45	C Flight continued its advance into Germany with 2nd Canadians, administrated by 660 AOP Squadron.	
1st May '45	Saw the squadron working on a front between Ede and Bude with 61st Super Heavy Regiment.	
4th May '45	(20.000 hrs) Squadron's last shoot of the campaign carried out by C Flight with the 61st Super Heavies against heavy AA emplacement near Emden.	
5th May '45	The day of the German surrender saw the squadron engaged in communications duties from Rostrup to Olderburg for Canadian Army HQ and 49th Div. HQ relieving 660 Sqd.	

7th Jun '45	661 Squadron moved back to Appledorn in Holland on communications duties with HQ 1st Canadians.
28th Jun '45	NJ 695 sent to 412 Repair and Salvage Unit after sustaining damage.
8th Jul '45	Squadron moved to Germany for communications work severing a connection of 1 year 8 months with HQ 1st Can. Army. C Flight at Syke under 51st Heavy Division.
12th Jul '45	NJ 965 returned to 661 Sqn. on communications duties with American 8th Army and 2nd Canadian Army.
1st Aug '45	661 Sqn. split between relief of 660 Sqd and the relief of 653 Sqd with the 7th Armoured Division.
6th Aug '45	C Flight move's to Itzhoe under command of 7th Armoured Div.
28th Aug '45	661 Sqn. moved back to Belgium on communications duties.
17th Oct '45	C Flight moved to join Sqd HQ at Ghent.
14th Nov '45	Returned to 20th Maintenance Unit.
8th Mar '46	Resold to Taylorcraft (England) Ltd. Later renamed Auster Aircraft Ltd., Thurmston, Leicester. Later sold in France as F-BEEJ. Returned to England in 1975 G-AJXV. Purchased virtually scrap in March 1977 and refurbished by present owners in Nottingham. CAA exemption from civil markings. Ministry of Defence permission for camouflage. This aircraft still has the original engine. Now owned and flown by P. Farries, Carlton, Nottingham.

Auster AOP Mk. IV NJ695 is currently owned by P. Farries of Carlton, Nottingham. (Bill Fisher).

Post war two military Auster models were built. The Model K, or Auster 6 in its AOP configuration or T Mk 7 and T Mk 10 when used in the trainer role and the B5 or Auster Mk 9 which was the last Auster type to enter military service. The Auster 6 was used by the British Army in Korea alongside types such as the American Bird Dog. It was also supplied to a number of overseas airarms including the South Africans, the Canadians and the Dutch. Although these air forces did not operate in a combat environment it

would enable restoration to a number of different colour schemes. After demobilisation many Mark 6s were converted as glider tugs whereas Mk 7s and Mk 10s tended to be converted to Beagle Terrier configuration with larger tail surfaces, soundproofing in the cabin, more luxurious seats and revised instrument panels and perspex layouts. It should however be possible to de-mod a Terrier back to Mk. 6 configuration if required.

Whereas the Mk. 6 had been a redesign of the Mk. V to take the Gipsy Major 7

engine of 145 hp with some beefing up of the structure, the Auster Mk 9 was a completely fresh design bearing no relationship to its C.G. Taylor origins. Gone were the wooden spars with metal ribs so similar to a Piper PA18 Supercub and gone were the bungees on the landing gear which were available from the US with a Piper part number. In their place came an entirely new wing with a single metal spar and metal leading edge D-box incorporating a split flap. The main and tail undercarriage incorporating Dowty liquid spring suspension with forged main legs and hydraulic brakes. The tail surfaces were of all metal construction and the engine used was the Blackburn Bombardier 209 developing 180 hp. This was one of the very first fuel injection engines under 200 hp. The Auster 9 incorporated provisions for an underwing survey camera and armour plating on the pilot's seat. The sideways facing seat of the Mk 5 and 6 was replaced by a rear seat which could be installed facing aft and 218 square feet of perspex gave excellent all round visibility. For operation in hot climates, the aircraft could be operated with the doors removed or the front windows could be opened through 90° to lie under the wing. About half a dozen Auster Mk 9s have found their way on to the UK register and three are to be found in the United States. Of these XN408 is probably the most interesting having been supplied to the Far East for anti-terrorist duties and passed to the Hong Kong Air Force when the British withdrew from Hong Kong. It is currently based in Florida as N408XN.

Purchase of a military Auster variant will guarantee that you become the owner of an aircraft of a type which has seen actual combat service. Selective purchase could result in you obtaining an airframe which has a documented combat history. The capital outlay for such a purchase is not excessive. Even allowing for the purchase of an aircraft in civilian configuration and recovering it

Auster Mk9. XR269/G-BDXY flying near Old Warden in Bedfordshire in 1969. (Bill Fisher).

and converting it to military colour scheme, the cost could probably be contained at less than £12,500 or US$25,000. This represents something like 7.5% of the asking price for a P-51D Mustang which rolled down the assembly line after

the end of World War II and probably had no significant military service history.

Warbirds Worldwide and the author can assist a potential purchaser who wishes to become the owner of this class of warbird. **WW** *M.D.N. Fisher.*

ROBERT TAYLOR

"HURRICANE SCRAMBLE"

A Limited Edition signed by four of Churchill's legendary FEW,
Bob Doe, 'Bee' Beamont, Peter Brothers and Denis Crowley-Milling

It is August 1940. The Battle of Britain is at its height. Great armadas of Luftwaffe aircraft have made incessant attacks on Southern Britain throughout the day. The unmistakeable roar of the Merlin engines fills the fighter station once again as the Hurricanes scramble into the air. It is their sixth operational sortie of the day. Such was the desperation of the Battle that it was commonplace for the young R.A.F. pilots to fly and fight from dawn to dusk during that hot summer of 1940. The redoubtable Hawker Hurricane bore the brunt of the operational combat flying during the epic Battle of Britain, accounting for no fewer than four fifths of air victories scored by the British fighter pilots. Without this wonderfully stable fighter aircraft, and the determination and courage of its young pilots, the battle would never have been won.

Robert Taylor's unique ability, together with his great knowledge of the subject gained by first-hand research and discussion with Battle of Britain pilots, has enabled him to paint this truly exceptional picture. In his inimitable and unmistakeable style, he has captured perfectly the atmosphere of the "Scramble", set in an airfield scene so typical of those frantic days in the summer of 1940. And each of the 1000 prints in the edition carries the original signatures of four famous Battle of Britain Aces, Bob Doe, DSO, DFC (leading living ace from the Battle of Britain) Bee Beamont, CBE, DSO, DFC, Peter Brothers, CBE, DSO, DFC, and Sir Denis Crowley-Milling, KCB, CBE, DSO, DFC. A truly historic collectors' print.

Print Size: 37″ × 26″   Price: £110.00 + £2.50 post.

THE MILITARY GALLERY

QUEENS PARADE PLACE, BATH, BA1 1NN
TEL: 0225-27521   FAX: 0225-446417

THE MILITARY GALLERY

QUEENS PARADE PLACE, BATH, BA1 1NN
TEL: 0225-27521   FAX: 0225-446417

Name . . . .
Address . . . .
. . . .
. . . .
Please mail . . . . copies of HURRICANE SCRAMBLE
☐ I enclose cheque for £112.50 inc. post
☐ Please charge my . . . . credit card

No: ☐☐☐☐☐☐☐☐☐☐☐☐☐☐☐☐☐☐

Expiry date . . . .   Signed . . . .
☐ Mail Colour Catalogue. I enclose £ . . . .
☐ Mail Free Copy of Military Gallery Newspaper
☐ Mail details of Dealer Programme (Trade only)

CA-16 Wirraway III A20-653 wearing the overall foliage green camouflage and white empennage and leading edges and carrying the No. 5 Squadron codes BF-F (which doubles as registration VH-BFF). Seen here flying over Wangaratta, Victoria. (Airworld Photographic Collection).

The Wirraway, an Australian aboriginal word meaning *Challenge*, was the first and indisputably the most famous product of the Commonwealth Aircraft Corporation. Although ordered as a general purpose type, Wirraways flew in every conceivable role from army co-operation aircraft to dive bomber, target marker and even fighter interceptor. But it is as a trainer that the Wirraway is best remembered. It formed the mainstay of the Royal Australian Air Force training programme throughout the war years and remained in service until 1959 at the Point Cook Flying Training School.

The Wirraway's production stemmed directly from Australia's traditional dependance upon the United Kingdom for its military and the majority of its civilian aircraft. The worsening European political situation of the early to mid 1930's brought with it the realization that Australia could not rely on England for military supplies, particularly in the event of war. To ensure that the RAAF would not be severely disadvantaged as a result of a European conflict, a consortium of Australia's foremost industrial companies formed the *Commonwealth Aircraft Corporation Pty. Ltd.*, on 17th October 1936. Prior to CAC's incorporation, a three man mission had been sent overseas to evaluate general purpose types considered suitable for production by the fledgling

company and this mission recommended the licence manufacture of the North American Aviation NA-26. North American offered two versions of the basic NA-26 design to Australia, the NA-32, (NA-16-1A), fitted with a fixed undercarriage and the NA-33, (NA-16-2K), fitted with a retractable undercarriage. Despite protests from within some sectors of the Australian Government for the choice of a non-British type, a production licence was obtained for the aircraft together with an example of each machine for further evaluation.

The NA-33 was eventually chosen, given the contract designation CA-1 by CAC and allocated the RAAF identification number A20. *CAC's* first contract called for the manufacture of forty CA-1 Wirraways, serialled A20-3 to A20-42, (A20-1 and A20-2 were allocated to the NA-32 and NA-33 respectively), and on 27th March 1939 the first production aircraft took to the air over *CAC's* Fishermen's Bend factory piloted by Flt. Lt. H. Boss-Walker.

Peter Anderson outlines the development and operational history of the Commonwealth Aircraft Corporation Wirraway general purpose aircraft.

Although externally similar to North American's AT-6 Texan due to their common ancestry, Wirraways vary considerably from their American counterpart. They were fitted with the locally produced geared version of the Pratt and Whitney R-1340 which drove a three blade propeller, the fuselage sides were fabric covered and armament consisted two fixed, fuselage-mounted, Vickers 0.303 machine guns firing through the propellor arc with a third mounted in the rear cockpit. Bombs could be carried under the centre section whilst a later version, the CA-16, was fitted with dive flaps and had provision for either 250 lb or 500 lb bombs on outer wing racks.

Under seven successive contracts 755 Wirraways were produced between 1939 and 1946 and these aircraft flew in every conceivable role, many far removed from even the widest interpretation of *General Purpose Aircraft*. When war broke out in the Pacific seven front line and three reserve units were equipped with Wirraways.

No. 21 Squadron RAAF, was deployed to Malaya in July 1940 with eighteen Wirraways but by November 1941 it had been re-equipped with the almost obsolete Brewster *Buffalo*. At that time the squadron's role also changed from general reconnaissance to that of a fighter unit although many of the pilots were totally inexperienced in fighter operations. To remedy this situation an

Part 1 *The Wonderful Wirraway*

advanced flying training unit was formed at Kluang with six Wirraways. Soon after the Japanese attack on Pearl Harbour and the concurrent landings in Malaya and the Philippines, these Wirraways found themselves in the thick of the fighting; utilised as dive bombers and even escorts for RAAF Hudsons and Martin B-10 bombers of the Netherlands East Indies Air Force.

Three thousand miles to the East, the Rabaul based Wirraways of No. 24 Squadron RAAF, bore the brunt of the Japanese advance through New Britain and New Ireland. On 6th January 1942, A20-137, piloted by Flt. Lt. B. Anderson gained the distinction of becoming the first RAAF aircraft to engage in air to air combat in the South West Pacific when it attacked a Kawanishi H6K *Mavis* flying boat over Rabaul. Acting as interceptors No. 24 Squadron's Wirraways fought valiantly against overwhelming odds but were soon decimated by the vastly superior Japanese fighters. On one occasion eight Wirraways took off to intercept a force of over 100 fighters and bombers attacking Rabaul. Although all but two of these Wirraways were either destroyed or severely damaged they continued to engage the enemy aircraft throughout their raid. One of the Japanese fighter pilots who participated in this attack spoke highly of the Australian pilots; ". . . we marvelled at their courage for they kept on attacking despite the incredibly superior numbers of Japanese fighters and the woeful inadequacy of the Australian equipment."

Despite the Wirraways stop-gap use as a fighter and dive bomber it was in its originally intended role of army co-operation aircraft that the type excelled. Both No. 4 and No. 5 Squadron RAAF employed Wirraways for target marking,

artillery spotting, photographic reconnaissance and supply, message and leaflet dropping from bases in the Solomon Islands, New Guinea and later Borneo, performing exceptional work in the support of Allied ground forces. The Wirraway's use in these widely varied duties gained it the reputation as a rugged and dependable workhorse. They often carried out their missions at or below tree top height in the face of heavy small arms fire and regularly returned to base with foliage embedded somewhere in the airframe.

Perhaps the most famous incident in the Wirraway's operational history occurred on 26th December 1942 when A20-103 piloted by F/O. J.S. Archer of No. 4 Squadron shot down a Mitsubushi A6M Reisen *Zeke* over Gona, New Guinea. No one was more suprised at this

turn of events than Archer himself and the signal that announced his victory reflected that amazement.

"Archer has shot down one Zeke, repeat one Zeke. Send six bottles beer."

The beer was sent (Castle Main XXXX? – Ed.) and A20-103 survived the war to be preserved by the Australian War Memorial in Canberra, the nation's capital.

In addition to its front line operational career, Wirraways served as advanced trainers for the duration of the war and continued as the RAAF's principal trainer until 1959 when they were finally supplanted by another CAC product, the Winjeel. Seventeen examples of the Wirraway were also used by the Royal Australian Navy Fleet Air Arm between 1948 and 1953. They were employed for both pilot and ground crew training at

Lower: (Hawker de Havilland Victoria Pty. Ltd) *Wirraways undergoing production at CAC's Fisherman's Bend factory. Forty-five Wirraways were being produced every month by September 1941.* **Below:** *A20-3, the first production Wirraway outside aircraft factory number one after return to CAC for rectification. Note the solid rubber rear tyre – an unusual feature for the type* (Hawker de Havilland Pty. Ltd.)

CAC CA-16 Wirraway III A20-649 at Point Cook RAAF Base, Melbourne, Victoria wearing the overall yellow training scheme but non-standard black anti-dazzle panel and canopy frame. December 1974 (Greg Banfield).

HMAS Albatross, the Navy's shore establishment at Nowra, New South Wales.

Very few Wirraways were used by civilian operators after the type was withdrawn from the RAAF due principally to the restrictions adopted towards military aircraft by the then Department of Civil Aviation. These restrictions effectively prohibited the operation of ex-military aircraft by civilians and as a result the vast majority of war surplus Australian aircraft, including Wirraways, were scrapped. A very small number of Wirraways were actually entered onto the Australian register of civil aircraft but these were company operated aircraft and were soon withdrawn from service. *CAC* did produce a highly modified version of the Wirraway called the *Ceres* to take advantage of surplus Wirraway airframes and large quantities of spares but only twenty were manufactured before production ceased. Understandably therefore almost all Wirraway survivors were confined to aviation museums or were purchased by farmers at disposal sales as a relatively inexpensive source of hardware for their farm machinery and buildings.

During the early 1970's a partial relaxation of the Government's restrictions concerning ex-military aircraft led to an increasing interest in the Wirraway. The type had a higher performance than the other wartime trainers then flying, and it was a genuine warbird with a fine operational history. Most important of all, it was within the financial reach of local enthusiasts. Fortunately, despite the wholesale post war scrap drives a significant number of Wirraways survived and it is even more fortunate that a substantial number of spares became available at the end of *Ceres* production. These airframes and spares have formed the basis of several planned and current rebuild projects, the first of which, A20-653 registered VH-BFF, flew at Moorabbin Airport, Melbourne, Victoria on 4th December 1975. In so doing it became the first ex-military aircraft to fly of Australia's modern *warbird* era.
WW Peter N. Anderson.

A number of CAC Wirraways are currently undergoing airworthy restoration in Australia, and in Part Two we will be looking at these, together with a listing of the known Wirraway survivors, a production listing and basic production details, general specifications, type variants and Royal Australian Fleet Air Arm aircraft.

The author acknowledges the assistance of Lt. Cdr. K. Alderman RAN, Mr. D. Baker of Hawker de Havilland (Victoria) Pty. Ltd. (formerly CAC), Mr. E. Field, Mr. R. Hourigan and Mr. P. Malone in the preparation of this article.

One of seventeen Wirraways allocated to the Royal Australian Navy for pilot and ground crew training at HMAS Albatross, NSW. Note the displaced roundel and yellow cowling markings (Australian Naval Aviation Museum).

Reno Update

Vendetta at Fort Wayne earlier this year. The Lear 23 jet wing is shown to advantage in this photograph. **Bottom:** *Note the modification to the fairing in the Lear horizontal stabilizer*

The 25th National Championship Air Races are being held at Reno between September 15th and 18th inclusive and it promises to be a memorable Silver Anniversary year with many new projects emerging to compete. The longest continuously running event of its kind anywhere in the world will feature all four classes of racing along with some of the most popular airshow acts in North America.

On the Unlimited side work continues to prepare John Sandberg's *Tsunami* in Minneapolis. This custom built Unlimited has been receiving a lot of attention of late and will be a real contender for this year's Unlimited Gold. Frank Sanders Sea Fury project is making rapid progress and promises to be good competition for the in-line engined Unlimited field. All eyes of course are on Tiger Destefani and *Strega* who pulled a win out of the hat last year, blasting the Sea Furies into oblivion. No doubt the workshops at Bakersfield are as busy as ever preparing the aircraft for a defence of the title.

Several YAK projects are currently underway and we will be covering these in our pre-race article in WW Number Six, along with our forecast for the winners in the Unlimited Gold, Silver and Bronze.

Vendetta

As we reported exclusively in Issue Two of WARBIRDS WORLDWIDE Tom Kelley and John Dilley of the *Fort Wayne Air Service* are building a very special racer utilising a Mustang fuselage and a Lear 23 mainplane. Butch Schroeder paid a recent visit to Fort Wayne, Indiana, to check on the project's progress ... 'I have to admit that I had some doubts when I first talked to John about the *Vendetta* project two years ago, but upon seeing one of the nicest, sleekest looking aircraft I have ever seen sat in the shops at Baer Field, my opinion has changed somewhat. The workmanship is of the highest standard and the roll-out and subsequent flight test programme are due to start very soon. John tells me that the aircraft, powered by a Jack Hovey Rolls-Royce 622 Merlin weighs in at well under 5600 lb and will be race ready at under 7400 lb. Drag versus horsepower computations have been completed and are projecting 533 mph at 300 hp at 5500 MSL with a stock propeller. With 1500 hp (57 inches manifold pressure and 3000 RPM) *Vendetta* is projected to go around the Reno pylons at close to 400 mph verses 359 mph in a stock Mustang.'

Blenheim Update

Bolingbroke RCAF 10201 in Canada prior to be shipped to Scotland. It now forms the basis for the BAM's new Blenheim project. (Dave Robertson via John Smith).

Michael Shreeve reports on the British Aerial Museum's Blenheim project now underway

The Blenheim is back! That well known sight at Duxford for so many years – a Bristol Blenheim on rebuild in the workshop known as *Blenheim Palace* will soon be evident again.

After last summer's triumphant flight and well publicised accident just four weeks later saw the destruction of G-MKIV during a flying display at Denham airfield. Graham Warner's *British Aerial Museum*, under the engineering direction of John Romain, had spent many years breathing life back into an abandoned hulk discovered on a Canadian farm and shipped to the UK in the early 1970s (see Warbirds Worldwide Number One). To have their prize snatched from them in their moment of triumph was indeed a cruel blow. Despite the tragedy, the *BAM* announced they would rebuild another Blenheim. Their ambition came a step nearer on Thursday 28th January when the Bolingbroke airframe, which will form the basis of the new project, arrived at Duxford. Like G-MKIV this aircraft is another Canadian built Bolingbroke Mk. IVT, consisting mainly of serial RCAF 10201 with

outer wing panels from serial 9703. It was purchased from Sir William Roberts Strathallen collection at Auchterarder in Scotland, having been shipped there from Canada in a dismantled state in mid 1984.

Parts from the damaged G-MKIV will also be used in the rebuild including, it is hoped, the majority of the required engine parts as well as the numerous smaller internal fittings and other parts.

At present, the *BAM* are completing the refurbishment of their Auster AOP. 9 XR241/G-AXRR and Chipmunk WP905/G-BNCZ is now awaiting airtesting. With these projects complete and the workshop re-organised and prepared, work will commence in the near future on the new project. It is anticipated that the rebuild will take considerably less time than the previous attempt due to the experience gained on the rebuild of G-MKIV, and a completion date three to five years hence is envisaged. In order to help meet the considerable costs involved the Blenheim Appeal (launched immediately after the accident) continues. Additionally, to provide a focus for the interest generated by

G-MKIV's all too brief flying career the *Blenheim Society* has been formed. Membership is open to all those with an interest in the type as well as former Blenheim crews. A highly successful inaugural meeting was held in the Officers' Mess building at Duxford last November with over 200 former Blenheim 'types' and enthusiasts present – many old friends being reunited for the first time since the war years. Although heavy fog prevented a planned flying demonstration by a P-40 the day was judged to be a great success by all attending. In particular John Smith's video of the rebuild and flying career of G-MKIV provided an excellent summary of the BAM team's achievements.

Warbirds Worldwide wishes the *British Aerial Museum* every success in their new project to provide a fitting tribute to all Blenheim crews. Membership details for the Blenheim Society and information regarding the appeal fund can be obtained from **The British Aerial Museum, Building 66, Duxford Airfield, Duxford, Cambs CB2 4QR, England.** WW *Michael Shreeve.*

WARBIRDS SCENE
WORLDWIDE

UNITED KINGDOM

Several of the fourteen warbirds mentioned in the Editorial in Issue Four have arrived here in the U.K. One of the most exciting British built warbirds to be purchased in the United States is the **Sea Fury FB11** 41H/ 609972 alias N232J which **Robert Lamplough** announced he has purchased from Bill Simms in Illinois in late April. The aircraft is painted in Royal Canadian Navy Colours and will be flown to Ohio to be hangared with Ron Runyan before being imported to the U.K. It will be especially nice to see an FB11 in civilian hands in Europe. Another scheduled arrival as we go to press is Anthony Haig-Thomas's **Grumman TBM-3E Avenger** N3966A which is due to arrive in the U.K. in July.

Warbirds of Great Britain took delivery of their **F4U-4** Corsair N4902 via Ipswich Docks on 19th February. The aircraft was towed to Ipswich airport by road and then flown into Biggin Hill. Just a few weeks later, as can be seen from the feature elsewhere in this issue, *The Old Flying Machine Company* took delivery of their **F4U-4** when Ray Hanna flew N240CA/Bu.No. 97513 into Duxford. A second addition to the OFMC fleet came quickly afterwards when their Grumman Avenger flew into their Cambridge base early in May.

Russ Snadden reports that the RAF Benson based **Messerschmitt Bf 109 G-2/Trop** Werknummer 10639 had the DB 605A engine installed in February; the Ministry of Defence are discussing the future of the aircraft at high level and a decision on this rare warbirds future will be made shortly. Rolls-Royce engineers John Rumbelow and Roger Slade installed the DB 605 engine and though some pipework needs to be manufactured the cowlings are now being fitted.

Top (J.S. Elcome) *The RAF Benson based Bf 109 G-2/Trop with its newly installed DB 605A engine.* **Lower** (Michael Shreeve) *Aces High are operating this B-25 Mitchell as a camera ship for* Piece of Cake. *It is seen here arriving at North Weald on 9th April.*

The only credible event that took place at North Weald on 9th April was the arrival of **B-25J-32NC Mitchell N1042B/44-30823** just after the incredible Wilkins & Wilkins auction. *Aces High* have been using the aircraft to film the air to air sequences for *Piece of Cake.* It is fitted with a much modified nose section to allow filming and is devoid of turrets of any kind.

Colour Captions Opposite: Top (Philip Wallick) *shows Bill Simms at the controls of Hawker Sea Fury FB11 N232J which is registered with construction number 41H-609972 has recently been purchased by North Weald based Robs Lamplough.* **Lower** (Denis Hersey) *see the report in CONTRAIL on this superb T.35 Vampire A79-636 taken near Laverton in March 1988.*

merly G-PSID which was recently registered as **F-AZFI** and is now based at La Ferte Alais. There is still a great deal of activity surrounding the YAK airframes (see the next issue for a full

a fast pace and there are two very important shows in France scheduled to take place. La Ferte Alais is the scene of the first which promises to be very exciting, and another show, scheduled

D-FMBB, four Mustangs, Eric Vormezeele's Fiat G46 OO-VOR, five Spitfires, the *Sabena Oldtimer's* Westland Lysander OO-SOT, the *Scandinavian Historic Flight's* A-26 Invader, the

allowed to land at Vitry on the 12th June provided prior notice is given by telephone on (France) 20 98 82 16.

Furious Pair

Sea Fury FB11 serial VW647 is now at HMAS Nowra being rebuilt to flying condition. Seen here being used by the Australian Department of Construction at an experimental building station where it was used to create hurricane force winds to test building structures. (Department of Construction via Peter Anderson).

This shot from British Aerospace shows an Iraqi Air Force Two-place Fury in full IAF markings – note the stencils are in English. Of particular interest are the individual bubble canopies rather without the bridge section used on the Royal Navy T.20s.